Written and Illustrated by Bill Ross

Thomas Nelson, Inc.
Nashville

Published in Nashville, Tennessee, by Tommy Nelson™, a division of Thomas Nelson, Inc.
Vice President of Children's Books: Laura Minchew; Editor: Tama Fortner;
Art Director: Karen Phillips

Bible stories are based on the *International Children's Bible, New Century Version,*
copyright © 1986, 1988 by Word Publishing. Used by permission.

Scripture followed by NKJV is taken from the *New King James Version.*
Copyright © 1982 by Thomas Nelson, Inc. Used by permission.
All rights reserved.

Library of Congress Cataloging-in-Publication Data

Ross, Bill, 1956–
    Hey, that's not what the Bible says! / written and illustrated by Bill Ross.
        p. cm.
    Summary: Tells a humorous, incorrect version of various Bible stories, and then corrects them and cites the chapter where the whole story can be read.
    ISBN 0-8499-5922-5
    1. Bible—Juvenile literature. [1. Bible stories.] I. Title.
BS539.R67 1999
220.9'505–dc21   98-51088
                                                                                                        CIP
                                                                                                        AC

Printed in the United States of America

99 00 01 02 03 WCT 9 8 7 6 5 4 3 2 1

**For my really cool daughters,
Kelly and Casey**

God created everything else.

Then God created Adam and Eve. Perfect people in a perfect world. The only thing God asked of Adam and Eve was that they not eat the fruit from a special tree.

So they didn't. And all the people of the world lived happily ever after, forever and ever!

THE END.

Okay, so Adam and Eve messed up. Satan tricked them, and they ate the fruit that God told them not to eat. That is when they first sinned. *Sin* is when we do something that we know God does not want us to do.

Turn to page 66 to read the real, true story of Adam and Eve from the Book of Genesis.

Years later, a whole bunch of people lived on the earth. The people wouldn't quit sinning. So God told a man named Noah to build a giant boat, called an ark.

All the people of the world got on Noah's ark. Then, God made it rain and rain. It was so boring on the ark that the people learned their lesson and never sinned again!

That's right. God told
Noah to put two of every kind of
animal inside the ark. Then
Noah and his family went inside,
too. Only Noah, his family, and the
animals were saved from the
great flood.

Turn to page 67 to read the real,
true *story of Noah's ark
from the Book of Genesis.*

One day, a man named Moses was busy tending sheep.

Just then, a mailman appeared with a letter from God. "Special delivery," the mailman said. "A letter for Mr. Moses."

In the letter, God explained that He couldn't remember Moses' phone number, so He had to write Moses His special message!

God really spoke to Moses as a voice coming from a burning bush. God told Moses to go and lead God's people out of Egypt!

Turn to page 68 to read the real, true *story of Moses and the burning bush* from the Book of Exodus.

Goliath was an angry, mean giant who hated God's people.
Goliath challenged any one of them to fight him, but they
were all too afraid.

Then, a very brave boy named David, who had been chosen by God, came forward to fight the giant. Goliath roared with laughter when he saw David.

But as David came closer, Goliath thought he knew him. The giant put on his giant glasses so that he could see David a little better.

"Hey!" Goliath shouted. "Aren't you David, son of Jesse? The one anointed by God? Can I have your autograph? Let's be friends!"

No, Goliath *never* wanted to be friends with David. In fact, Goliath was so mean and hated God's people so much, that he wanted to make them his slaves. But David took a smooth stone, put it in his sling, and killed the giant. God had used David to save His people.

Turn to page 70 to read the real, true story of David and Goliath from the Book of 1 Samuel.

Once there was a man named Daniel who loved God. Daniel loved to pray to God. But praying to God was against the law in the land where Daniel lived.

But Daniel prayed anyway. So he was arrested and thrown into a den of big, hairy, hungry lions!

Before the lions ate Daniel, they put ketchup and mustard on his head.

That's right! God sent His angel to shut the lions' mouths. Daniel was not hurt by the lions because he believed in God!

Turn to page 71 to read the real, true story of Daniel and the lions' den from the Book of Daniel.

God chose Jonah to go to Nineveh and tell the people there to obey Him. But Jonah didn't want to do it.

Jonah ran from God. "I'll get on a ship and go to the middle of the ocean," said Jonah. "God will never find me there!"

So Jonah never had to do what God wanted him to do.

Jonah couldn't hide from God; God is everywhere. God made a huge storm. The ship nearly sank. So the sailors threw Jonah into the ocean, because they knew God was angry with him.

A giant fish swallowed Jonah. God kept Jonah safe inside the fish while Jonah prayed, "Thank You, God, for saving me. I'm sorry that I ran from You."

After three days, God made the giant fish spit Jonah out onto the beach. Then Jonah went to Nineveh as God had asked. Jonah learned that it is better to obey God the *first* time.

Turn to page 72 to read the real, true *story of Jonah and the big fish from the Book of Jonah.*

Joseph and Mary were going to get married. Angels visited them and said, "Mary is going to have a baby. This baby is from God! You will name Him Jesus because He will save the people from their sins!"

About the time that Mary's baby was to be born, Joseph and Mary had to travel to Bethlehem.

Of course, since Mary's baby was the Son of God—the Savior of the world—she went to the biggest, shiniest, cleanest, best hospital in all the land!

Actually, there was no room *anywhere* for Joseph and Mary to stay. So they went to a stable, a place for animals. There, Mary gave birth to baby Jesus, the Son of God, the Savior of the world!

Turn to page 74 to read the real, true *story of the birth of Jesus from the Book of Luke.*

Jesus grew up, and He began to teach people about God. One evening, after teaching all day, Jesus got into a boat with His closest friends and He took a nap.

A wild storm came, and waves crashed against the boat.
Jesus' friends were frightened. They woke Jesus up.
"Save us, Jesus! Or we'll drown!" they screamed.

Jesus quickly reached down, found the secret control panel, and flipped the secret power switch. Instantly the little fishing boat was transformed into a watertight, nuclear-powered, New Testament submarine!

Jesus simply spoke to the storm. He said, "Be still," and all was calm. His friends were amazed when they saw that Jesus could control the weather.

Turn to page 75 to read the real, true *story of Jesus calming the storm from the Book of Mark.*

Some people didn't believe that Jesus was the Son of God.
They wanted Jesus killed for saying such a crazy thing.

Soldiers arrested Jesus and led Him away to be crucified on a wooden cross.

Suddenly, Jesus turned into Super-Duper-Mega-Jesus and beat up the soldiers!

No, Jesus didn't beat up anyone. He didn't even try to get away. Jesus died on the cross for our sins, so that we can live with Him in heaven forever.

Turn to page 76 to read the real, true story of the crucifixion of Jesus from the Book of John.

After Jesus was killed, He was buried in a tomb. A giant, round stone was rolled in front of the entrance.

Three days later, the workers came with a giant crane and put in a nice tombstone to mark the place where Jesus was buried.

Three days after Jesus died, some of His followers went to the tomb. But the rock had been rolled away, and the tomb was empty. Jesus had risen from the dead—just as He had said He would!

Turn to page 78 to read the real, true story of the resurrection of Jesus from the Book of Matthew.

God wants us to be perfect—just like Jesus. But we can't be perfect, because—like Adam and Eve—we all sin. In order to live with God and Jesus in heaven, we need to be perfect. But how can we ever be perfect if we sin? The good news is that God can forgive us. Then we can be perfect in God's eyes. That's why Jesus, God's Son, died on the cross—for us. Jesus received the punishment for our sins, so that we can be forgiven.

You can pray to Jesus and thank Him for saving you from your sins. Thank Him for being your Savior! Remember, Jesus rose from the dead and lives with God in heaven. He always hears you when you pray!

For God so loved the world that He gave His only begotten Son, that whoever believes in Him should not perish but have everlasting life.

–John 3:16 NKJV

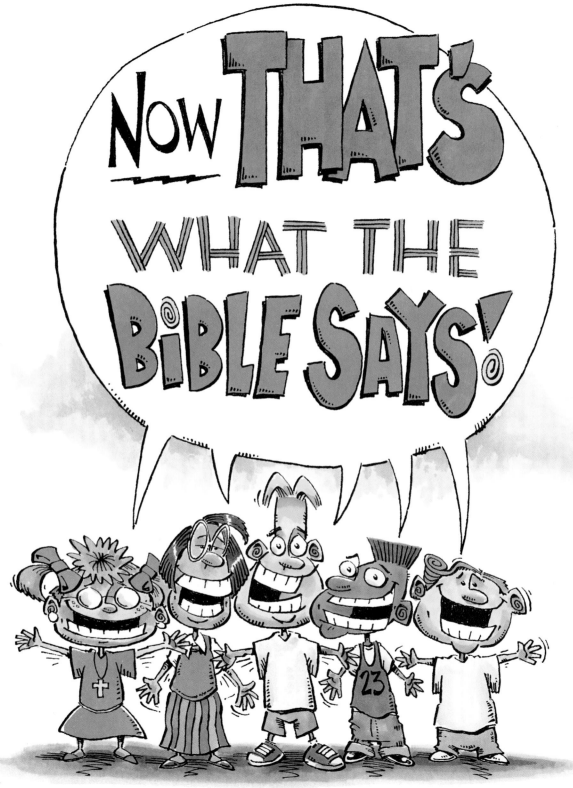

The real, *true* stories . . .

Adam and Eve

In the beginning, God made the earth and the sky. But the earth was empty and dark. So God made the light, and there was day and night. Next He made water and land. He filled the earth with plants, fish, birds, and animals. God then made the most wonderful creatures of all—He made a man and a woman in His own likeness. They were called Adam and Eve.

God planted a beautiful garden called Eden. And in the garden, God put every kind of tree that was good for food. Then God put Adam and Eve in the garden to live there and to care for it. God only had one rule in the garden. "You must not eat fruit from the tree that gives knowledge of good and evil," God said. "If you ever eat that fruit, you will die."

One day, the snake—who was really the devil—spoke to Eve. "Eat the fruit," the snake said. "You will not die. You will learn about good and evil. Then you will be like God." Eve believed the snake's lie, so she ate some of the fruit. Eve also gave some to Adam, and he ate it. Adam and Eve then heard God walking in the garden. They were afraid, so they hid from God.

But God knew what Adam and Eve had done. He punished them by making them leave the garden. They would now have to work hard for their food. They would grow old. And one day, they would die, just as God had said.

From the Book of Genesis, chapters one, two, and three.

Noah's Ark

There were now many people living on the earth, but everyone had become bad. Even all their thoughts were evil. But Noah was a good man, and he pleased God. One day God said to Noah, "People have made the earth full of violence, so I am going to flood the earth. I will destroy everyone and everything. But I will save you and your family. You must build a big boat."

God told Noah how to build the boat, which was called an ark, and Noah did as God said. God sent two of every kind of animal and bird to Noah. Noah herded them all into the ark. Noah, his wife, his sons, and his sons' wives also went inside the ark and closed the door. Then it started to rain!

It rained for 40 days and 40 nights. The water got deeper and deeper, until even the mountains were covered. Everything on earth was destroyed. Only Noah, his family, and the animals on the ark were saved. They were safe because Noah had obeyed God.

At last the rain stopped. Noah sent a dove out to find dry ground. But the dove could not find a place to land, so it came back. A week later, Noah sent the dove out again. This time it brought back a small olive leaf. The earth was almost dry! The next week when Noah sent out the dove, it didn't come back.

Now Noah, his family, and all the animals could leave the ark. God put a beautiful rainbow in the sky as a sign of His promise never again to destroy the earth with water.

From the Book of Genesis, chapters six, seven, eight, and nine.

Moses and the Burning Bush

God's people, the Israelites, were living in Egypt. But there were so many Israelites that the king of Egypt feared they might take Egypt away from him. So he made the Israelites his slaves. Then, to keep the Israelites from growing in number, the evil king made a law that said all Israelite baby boys must be thrown into the Nile River.

So when one of the Israelite women gave birth to a son, she hid him. But after three months, she could not hide him any longer. She covered a basket with tar so that it would float, and she put the baby in the basket. She then put the basket in the Nile River.

When the king's daughter went down to the river to take a bath, she found the basket with the baby boy inside. He was crying, and the king's daughter felt sorry for him. "This is one of the Israelite babies," she said. She adopted the baby as her own son and named him Moses, because she had pulled him out of the water. So, Moses grew up in the house of the king of Egypt.

One day, after Moses had become a man, he saw an Egyptian beating an Israelite slave. Moses became angry and killed the Egyptian. When the king heard what Moses had done, he tried to have Moses killed. But Moses ran away from Egypt and went to the land of Midian.

As Moses was resting near a well in Midian, some girls came to water their father's sheep. But some shepherds also came, and they chased the girls away. Moses defended the girls and watered their sheep for them. He was then taken to meet the girls' father, Jethro, a Midianite priest. Jethro thanked Moses for helping his daughters. Moses agreed to stay with them in Midian, and Jethro's daughter Zipporah became Moses' wife.

One day, as Moses was taking care of Jethro's sheep, he saw something very strange. It was a bush that was on fire, but it was not burning up! Moses went over to look at the bush. As he neared it, a voice spoke to him from the bush. It was God! "Do not come any closer!" God said. "Take off your sandals. You are standing on holy ground." Moses covered his face because he was afraid to look at God.

God said, "I have seen My people, the Israelites, suffering in Egypt. Go to the king of Egypt and tell him to let My people leave." When Moses heard God's plan, he was sure he couldn't do what God was asking. But God told him, "I will be with you." God then gave him miraculous signs to show the Israelite people that God was with Moses. God also sent for Moses' brother Aaron to help him. So Moses went back to Egypt to lead God's people out of slavery.

From the Book of Exodus, chapters one, two, three, and four.

David and Goliath

The Israelites were at war with the Philistines. One of the Philistine soldiers was named Goliath. He was a giant of a man. Goliath shouted to the Israelite soldiers, "Choose a man and send him to fight me. If he can kill me, we will become your servants. But if I kill him, you will become our servants." When the Israelites heard Goliath's words, they were very afraid.

David was a young shepherd who had brought food for his brothers in the Israelite army. When he heard Goliath's words, David was not afraid. "I will go and fight this Philistine!" he said.

Saul, the king of the Israelites, called David to him. "You can't fight Goliath," Saul told David. "You're only a boy, and Goliath is a giant warrior."

But David's faith in God was great. "God has saved me from lions and bears while I was tending my father's sheep," said David. "God will save me from this Philistine."

Saul offered David his own armor, but David did not want it. He went to fight Goliath with only a sling and five smooth stones. When Goliath saw that David was only a small boy, he laughed. But David put a stone in his sling and slung it at Goliath. The stone hit Goliath in the head and knocked him down. Then David took Goliath's sword and killed him. When the Philistines saw that Goliath was dead, they turned and ran.

From the Book of 1 Samuel, chapter seventeen.

Daniel and the Lions' Den

Daniel loved God very much, and he prayed to Him three times a day, every day. Daniel was also one of the leaders in King Darius's kingdom. When Daniel showed that he could do the work better than the other leaders, King Darius chose Daniel to help lead the kingdom. The other leaders were very jealous. These bad men thought of a way to get rid of Daniel. They tricked King Darius into making a terrible law. This law said that people could pray only to King Darius for thirty days. Anyone who broke this law would be thrown into a den of lions!

Daniel heard about the new law, but he still prayed to God. The bad men told King Darius. The king now saw the bad men's trick. He tried to think of a way to save Daniel, but even the king could not change a law after it had been made. Sadly, King Darius had Daniel arrested and thrown into the lions' den.

Early the next morning, King Darius hurried to the lions' den. As he came near the den, he called out, "Daniel, servant of the living God! Has the God that you always worship been able to save you from the lions?"

"Yes!" Daniel answered. "God sent His angel to close the lions' mouths. They have not hurt me."

King Darius was very happy. He told his servants to lift Daniel out of the lions' den and to throw the bad men in! Then King Darius made a new law that said everyone was to worship the God of Daniel.

From the Book of Daniel, chapter six.

Jonah and the Big Fish

One day, God spoke to Jonah, "Go to Nineveh and preach to the people there, for they have become very wicked."

But Jonah did not want to go to Nineveh and preach, so he tried to run away from God. Jonah went down to the city of Joppa. There he found a ship that was going far away from Nineveh. Jonah paid for the trip and went aboard.

But God sent a great wind. The wind made the sea very rough, so that the ship was about to break apart. The sailors were afraid. Each man cried out to his own god to save them.

Jonah had gone down into the ship, where he had lain down and fallen asleep. The captain went to him and said, "How can you sleep? Get up and pray to your God! Maybe He will save us!"

Jonah told the sailors that he was trying to run away from God, and that it was his fault that God had sent the storm. The sea got rougher and rougher. "What can we do to make the sea calm?" the sailors asked Jonah.

"Throw me into the sea," Jonah said, "and it will become calm."

But the sailors did not want to throw Jonah into the sea to die. They did their best to row the ship back to land, but the wind and sea became even wilder. The sailors cried out to God to forgive them, and then they threw Jonah overboard. The sea became calm.

God sent a big fish to swallow Jonah. Jonah was inside the fish for three days and three nights. All that time he prayed and thanked God for saving him from drowning. And Jonah promised to start obeying God. Then God spoke to the fish, and the fish spit Jonah out of its stomach onto dry land.

God said to Jonah again, "Get up and go preach to the people of Nineveh."

This time, Jonah obeyed God. He got up and went to Nineveh. He told the people, "God is angry with you. If you don't change your ways, God will destroy Nineveh!"

The people of Nineveh believed in God, and they believed Jonah's message from God. They stopped eating for a while, and they put on rough cloth to show how sad they were. Even the king declared that all the people should stop doing bad things. When God saw how the people of Nineveh had changed, He did not punish them.

From the Book of Jonah.

The Birth of Jesus

Mary was a young girl who was engaged to Joseph from the family of David. One day, God sent His angel Gabriel to visit Mary. Gabriel said, "God is pleased with you. You will give birth to a son, and you will name Him Jesus. God will give Him the throne of King David, and His kingdom will never end."

"How will this happen?" Mary asked.

The angel said, "The Holy Spirit will come upon you. The baby will be holy and He will be called the Son of God."

When it was almost time for Mary's baby to be born, Augustus Caesar ordered that everyone be counted in a census. Mary and Joseph traveled to Bethlehem to be counted. In Bethlehem, the time came for Mary to have the baby. There was no room for them in the inn, so Mary and Joseph stayed in a stable. There, Mary gave birth to the baby Jesus. She wrapped Him with cloths and laid Him in a manger, which was the animals' feeding box.

That night, some shepherds were watching their sheep in a nearby field. Suddenly, God's angel appeared to them and said, "Don't be afraid. I am bringing you good news. Today your Savior was born in Bethlehem! He is Christ the Lord. You will find Him wrapped in cloths and lying in a manger."

The shepherds hurried to Bethlehem. They found the baby just as the angel had said. The shepherds praised God for all they had seen and heard!

From the Book of Luke, chapters one and two.

Jesus Calms the Storm

Jesus grew up and began teaching the people about God. Great crowds gathered to hear Him everywhere He went.

One evening, after teaching the people, Jesus said to His closest followers (who were called disciples), "Come with Me across the lake." So He and the disciples left the crowds of people and got into a boat. While they were on the lake, a very strong wind began to blow. The waves began coming over the sides of the boat and filling it with water. Jesus was asleep at the back of the boat. The disciples went to Him and woke Him. "Teacher," they shouted, "don't You care about us? We're going to drown!"

Jesus stood up and commanded the wind and the waves to stop. "Quiet! Be still!" He said. The wind stopped, and the lake became calm.

Jesus asked His disciples, "Why are you afraid? Do you still have no faith?"

The disciples were very afraid. "What kind of man is this?" they asked one another. "Even the wind and the waves obey Him!"

From the Book of Mark, chapter four.

Jesus Is Crucified

There were some of the Jewish leaders who did not believe that Jesus was who He said He was, the Son of God.

One night, while Jesus was praying in the garden, He was betrayed by Judas, one of His own disciples. Judas led the soldiers to Jesus, and they arrested Him. They took Jesus to the Jewish high priest. The high priest asked Jesus questions about His disciples and His teaching. They did not like Jesus' answers, so they hit Him.

The Jewish leaders then took Jesus to the palace of Pilate, the Roman governor. They asked Pilate to have Jesus killed. Pilate questioned Jesus, but he could not find a reason to kill Him. Pilate wanted to let Jesus go free, but the Jews shouted, "No!"

Pilate ordered that Jesus be taken away and whipped. The soldiers used thorny branches to make a crown. They put this crown on Jesus' head and put a purple robe around Him. Then the soldiers said, "Hail! King of the Jews!" And they hit Jesus in the face.

Again Pilate tried to free Jesus. But the Jewish leaders kept shouting, "Kill Him on a cross!" Finally, Pilate turned Jesus over to them to be killed.

The soldiers made Jesus carry His own cross. They took Him to a hill outside of Jerusalem called Golgotha, which means "The Place of the Skull." There the soldiers nailed Jesus to the cross. Two other men were also hung on crosses, one on each side of Jesus.

Jesus' mother and some other women stood near His cross. Jesus saw His mother and His disciple John there also. Jesus asked John to take care of His mother. Then He said, "I am thirsty." The soldiers soaked a sponge in vinegar, put the sponge on a branch of a hyssop plant, and lifted it to Jesus' mouth. Jesus tasted the vinegar. "It is finished," Jesus said, and He bowed His head and died.

Later, a man named Joseph from Arimathea asked Pilate if he could take the body of Jesus. (Joseph was a secret follower of Jesus. He had kept it a secret because he was afraid of the Jews.) Pilate gave him permission to take Jesus' body down from the cross. Joseph and his friend Nicodemus took Jesus' body away. They wrapped His body with many spices in pieces of linen cloth. Then they put Jesus' body in a tomb in a garden near where He had been killed.

From the Book of John, chapters eighteen and nineteen.

Jesus Lives!

Early on the first day of the week, Mary Magdalene and another woman named Mary went to Jesus' tomb.

There was a strong earthquake, and an angel of the Lord came down from heaven. The angel went to the tomb and rolled the stone away from its entrance. Then the angel sat on the stone. He shone as bright as lightning and his clothes were as white as snow. The soldiers guarding the tomb were frightened of the angel. They shook with fear and then became like dead men.

But the angel said to the women, "Don't be afraid. I know that you are looking for Jesus, the One who was killed on the cross. But He is not here. He has risen from death just as He said He would. Look and see the place where His body was. Then go quickly and tell His followers that Jesus has risen from death. He is going into Galilee, and He will be there before you. You will see Him there."

The women quickly left the tomb. They were frightened, but they were also very happy. They hurried to tell Jesus' followers what had happened. Suddenly, Jesus met them and said, "Greetings." The women went to Jesus, held His feet, and worshiped Him. Then Jesus said to them, "Don't be afraid. Go and tell My brothers to go to Galilee. They will see Me there."

From the Book of Matthew, chapter twenty-eight.